SKOKIE PUBLIC LIBRARY

3 1232 00960 7732

D1376883

DREAM JOBS IN
MANUFACTURING

ADRIANNA MORGANELLI

CRABTREE
PUBLISHING COMPANY
WWW.CRABTREEBOOKS.COM

CUTTING-EDGE CAREERS IN TECHNICAL EDUCATION

Author:
Adrianna Morganelli

Series research and development:
Reagan Miller

Editorial director:
Kathy Middleton

Editor:
Petrice Custance

Proofreader:
Lorna Notsch

Design, photo research, and prepress:
Katherine Berti

Print and production coordinator:
Katherine Berti

Photographs:
Free Range Stock
   Thomas Adomaitis: p. 15 (bottom)
iStockphoto
   andresr: p. 6
   Richard-7: p. 12 (bottom left)
NASA: p. 11 (center left)
Shutterstock
   aapsky: p. 9 (center)
   BlackMac: p. 26 (bottom left)
   Grigvovan: p. 20 (bottom)
   Stoyan Yotov: p. 8 (bottom)
Stelfab Niagara Ltd.: p. 11 (bottom)
All other images by Shutterstock

Library and Archives Canada Cataloguing in Publication

Morganelli, Adrianna, 1979-, author
      Dream jobs in manufacturing / Adrianna Morganelli.
(Cutting-edge careers in technical education)
Includes index.
Issued in print and electronic formats.
ISBN 978-0-7787-4439-9 (hardcover).--
ISBN 978-0-7787-4450-4 (softcover).--
ISBN 978-1-4271-2030-4 (HTML)
      1. Manufacturing industries--Vocational guidance--Juvenile literature.
2. Manufacturing industries--Employees--Training of--Juvenile literature.
I. Title.
HD9720.5.M77 2018   j670.23   C2018-900259-X
                                             C2018-900260-3

Library of Congress Cataloging-in-Publication Data

Available at the Library of Congress

Crabtree Publishing Company

www.crabtreebooks.com   1-800-387-7650

Printed in the U.S.A./052018/CG20180309

Copyright © 2018 CRABTREE PUBLISHING COMPANY. All rights reserved. No part of this publication may be reproduced, stored in a retrieval system or be transmitted in any form or by any means, electronic, mechanical, photocopying, recording, or otherwise, without the prior written permission of Crabtree Publishing Company. In Canada: We acknowledge the financial support of the Government of Canada through the Canada Book Fund for our publishing activities.

Published in Canada
Crabtree Publishing
616 Welland Ave.
St. Catharines, Ontario
L2M 5V6

Published in the United States
Crabtree Publishing
PMB 59051
350 Fifth Avenue, 59th Floor
New York, New York 10118

Published in the United Kingdom
Crabtree Publishing
Maritime House
Basin Road North, Hove
BN41 1WR

Published in Australia
Crabtree Publishing
3 Charles Street
Coburg North
VIC 3058

CONTENTS

INTRODUCTION TO CTE

Do you like building things? Do you love the challenge of figuring out how something works? Do you dream of helping people look or feel better? Career and Technical Education can lead you toward an exciting and fullfilling career.

Career and Technical Education (CTE) programs combine academic studies, such as math and science, with valuable hands-on training. CTE students develop job-specific skills that are in high demand by employers. CTE programs are divided into 16 career clusters. Some examples of these career clusters are Information Technology, Human Services, Arts and Communications, Business Management and Administration, Manufacturing, and Hospitality and Tourism. Each CTE career cluster is divided into job pathways. Each job pathway is a grouping of jobs that require similar interests and paths of study. For example, in the Information Technology career cluster, the Network Systems pathway includes jobs such as communications analyst and information technology engineer.

DID YOU KNOW?

SkillsUSA and Skills Canada promote CTE programs in middle and high schools. Both organizations offer competitions for students across all CTE career clusters at both the state/provincial and national levels.

Landscape architects work with government departments, city planners, engineers, and private landowners to plan city parks and green spaces. They also work to shape environmental safety policies. This architect is using a theodolite, which is a piece of equipment used to measure angles while **surveying** land.

These **apprentices** are training on a computer numerical control (CNC) machine.

WHY CTE?

Behind every **innovation** is a creative thinker who loves a challenge. Employers are looking for people who can look at problems in new or different ways. This is what CTE is all about. By 2020, around 10 million new skilled workers will be needed in the United States alone. This huge demand means there are many great opportunities out there for you.

There is a wide variety of exciting CTE careers. Check out the introductory programs that are offered in your area. Most high schools offer a wide variety of CTE programs, and even some middle schools have them. But you don't have to choose a career right now. This is your time to explore!

APPRENTICESHIPS

Depending on what job interests you, you may be eligible to become an apprentice. This means you are able to learn the skills of a profession and practice these skills in the real world at the same time. As an added incentive, apprentices get paid while they learn, too! Apprenticeships are available in many industries, including construction, health care, and manufacturing.

It is estimated that more than two billion people around the world play video games—and that number is expected to grow. That means there are many opportunities for game designers!

MANUFACTURING

Nearly every product we use, including items essential to everyday life, is designed and created within the manufacturing industry.

Careers in manufacturing involve the planning, managing, and processing of **raw materials** into finished goods that are sold and used. Have you ever wondered what it would be like to be responsible for shipping goods to consumers all over the world? Then perhaps a career as a **logistics** engineer is a perfect fit for you. If you enjoy putting models together, such as model cars or airplanes, becoming an assembler is a career option. The job possibilities in manufacturing are as endless as the items you can create!

MANUFACTURING JOB PATHWAYS:

PRODUCTION	People in these jobs make and assemble parts.
MANUFACTURING PRODUCTION PROCESS	Employees design products and monitor the manufacturing process of products.
MAINTENANCE, INSTALLATION, AND REPAIR	These careers include making sure machines, tools, and equipment are in good and safe working order.
QUALITY ASSURANCE	Workers ensure proper procedures are followed.
LOGISTICS AND INVENTORY CONTROL	People in these careers ship raw materials and finished products around the world.
HEALTH, SAFETY, AND ENVIRONMENTAL ASSURANCE	Workers create programs and conduct inspections to ensure employee and environmental safety.

HOW TO USE THIS BOOK

Each two-page spread focuses on a specific career in the Manufacturing CTE cluster. For each career, you will find a detailed description of life on the job, advice on the best educational path to take (see right), and tips on what you can do right now to begin preparing for your dream job.

KEEPING YOUR OPTIONS OPEN

As you navigate your way through the career paths in this book, it is important that you keep your mind open to different job possibilities. We are always changing, and your interests may evolve over time. For this reason, it is a good idea not to limit yourself to studying one specific field, but instead, surge ahead with researching many different jobs.

YOUR PATH

SECONDARY SCHOOL

This section lists the best subjects to take in high school.

POST-SECONDARY

Some jobs require an apprenticeship and **certification** while others require a college or university degree. This section gives you an idea of the best path to take after high school.

DID YOU KNOW?

There are currently 12.5 million Americans working in manufacturing. Over the next decade, it is estimated that there will be 3.5 million job openings in the industry.

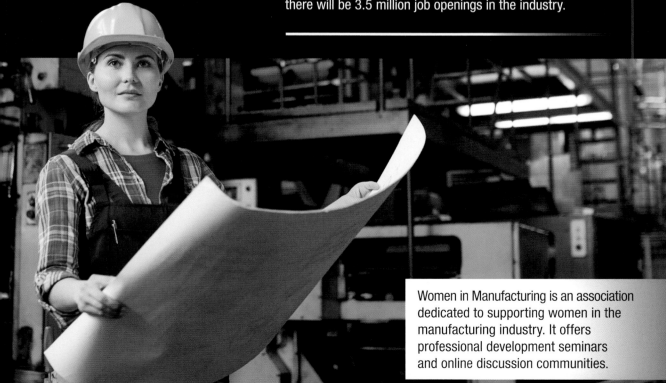

Women in Manufacturing is an association dedicated to supporting women in the manufacturing industry. It offers professional development seminars and online discussion communities.

ASSEMBLER

Before we can use a product, it has to be assembled, or put together. Toys, cars, household items such as toasters, and even aircraft are put together by workers called assemblers.

As an assembler, you will be putting together the pieces of one component, or part, of a product, or you may work to assemble a finished product. You will be working with your hands, but also with robots and computers to get your job done. This way, the assembly process is quicker and often more precise. Jobs in assembly vary greatly depending on the product that is being made.

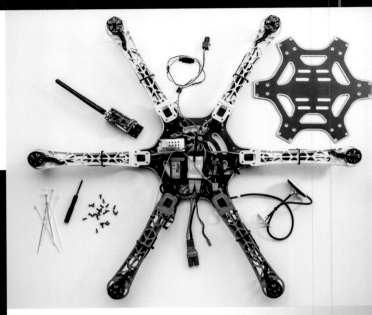

Would you be interested in putting this drone together? If you are, then you should consider becoming an assembler!

Some high-tech components that assemblers work on can be damaged by even the slightest bit of dust. In these cases, a **sterile** work environment is essential.

The ability to read plans and **blueprints** is an important part of an assembler's job.

YOUR PATH TO WORK AS AN ASSEMBLER

SECONDARY SCHOOL

Math, science, computer, technology, and CTE electronics courses are a great start.

POST-SECONDARY

A college degree in manufacturing or a related field is advised.

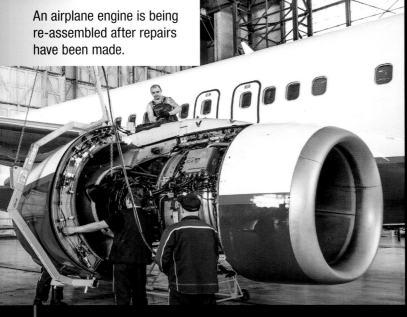

An airplane engine is being re-assembled after repairs have been made.

ON THE JOB

Assemblers need to be able to read and understand assembly instructions, manuals, and blueprints. They use **templates** and read measurements to properly position the parts that are to be assembled. They are responsible for ensuring that the components or products that they are working on meet the necessary specifications. If they don't, assemblers have to identify what is wrong in order for the assembly team to create the correct finished product.

WHAT CAN YOU DO NOW?

Put together your own toys! The next time an adult offers to put something together for you, say "No, thank you." Practice reading and following assembly instructions. Ask for permission, and then take apart a toy or device and see if you can put it back together.

Some assembly jobs require repetitive motions, such as regularly lifting or moving items, so assemblers need a lot of stamina!

9

WELDER

Welding is a complex and challenging profession, and also one that never gets boring. With more than 100 different welding processes, the manufacturing possibilities are endless.

Welders use special machines that create intense heat to cut and weld, or join, materials such as metals and **alloys**. They follow specific designs or blueprints to create many products, including automobiles, storage containers, and ships. After pieces are shaped and welded together, they smooth and polish the metal surfaces. Welders are also responsible for performing maintenance checks on their equipment to ensure it is in good working order. Welders should have good mathematical skills, as they need to calculate the dimensions of the parts to be welded.

ON THE JOB

As welders must work with dangerous tools, they must be diligent in following all of the safety rules of their workplace, including wearing the personal protective equipment they are supplied. If you decide to become a welder, you will need to be focused on your tasks, because distractions could lead to serious injury. Welders must pay attention to detail and stay current with new welding processes and equipment.

More than 50 percent of all products required welding during manufacturing.

WHAT CAN YOU DO NOW?

Research the different processes and types of equipment used for welding. Watch video tutorials online to learn more. Get used to working with your hands (and make some adults happy!) by asking to do jobs around the house such as vacuuming or gardening.

YOUR PATH TO WORK AS A WELDER

SECONDARY SCHOOL

Math, science, technology, and CTE construction courses are a great start.

POST-SECONDARY

College programs and certification are available.

How would you like to work in space? The International Space Station could not have been built without welders.

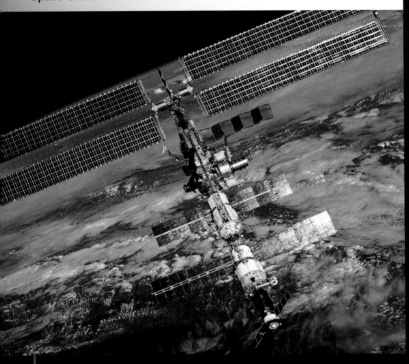

After welding, an angle grinder is used to smooth and polish the item.

DID YOU KNOW?

Much of the world's landfill waste consists of **drums** and other packaging. As a result, many companies manufacture containers that are recyclable and reusable. One such company is Stelfab Niagara Inc., from Ontario, Canada. This company manufactures **intermediate bulk containers (IBCs)** made of steel for use all over the world in the agricultural, **petrochemical**, and pharmaceutical industries. Once the bins' pieces are cut from carbon or stainless steel sheets, welders begin joining the pieces together to form bins that will hold chemicals, food products, lubricants, oils, and paints.

TOOL AND DIE MAKER

Traditionally, tool and die makers only used mechanical equipment to create parts for the manufacturing industry. Today, they also use computers to do some of the work.

Tool and die makers cut, shape, and finish tools made of metal that are used to produce products. Some common tools that they make include **milling cutters**, tool bits, **jigs**, and even entire machines that manufacture different products. They also make dies, which are special metal blocks that cut or shape materials, such as plastic, sheet metal, and even food. These dies are forged, which means they are made by heating the metal in a furnace or fire, or sometimes by hammering them into shape. Many items are made with dies, from complicated computer pieces and automobile parts to a simple paper clip.

Tool and die makers are needed to make machinery, **hardware**, and parts for aircraft and motor vehicles.

ON THE JOB

If you decide to become a tool and die maker, you will be working from engineered drawings and will need to create these designs using computer-aided design (CAD) software. After marking the designs on the metal, you will cut it to size and shape it using machines and hand tools. Tool and die makers need to be precise in their work. They must make necessary adjustments to their machinery to control the speed, material feed, and cut locations, and they make sure the machines are working properly. Once a product is complete, they are responsible for inspecting it to ensure that there are no defects and that it is a quality product.

A metal die used for making fresh fusilli Italian pasta. The dough is forced through the holes to produce the coiled noodles.

This tool and die maker programs a computer that will direct a machine to cut steel in a specific way to create a milling cutter.

YOUR PATH TO WORK AS A TOOL AND DIE MAKER

SECONDARY SCHOOL

Focus on math, science, computer, technology, and CTE manufacturing classes.

POST-SECONDARY

An apprenticeship program is required.

WHAT CAN YOU DO NOW?

Research processes and techniques for tool and die making. Learn about computer-aided design. Ask your teacher if a factory tour can be arranged for your class to be able to see machinists working in person.

When cutting metal, machines are controlled either by a computer program or manually by the machinist.

A variety of milling cutters.

INDUSTRIAL PAINTER

As an industrial painter, your job is to paint finished manufactured goods—these could be anything from small metal toolboxes to the enormous **hulls** of ships.

ON THE JOB

The first duty of an industrial painter is to prepare the surface to be painted, which could be metal, wood, or plastic. Any previous finishes are removed with chemicals or by **sandblasting**, and the surfaces are cleaned and left to dry. Industrial painters prepare their paint using measuring equipment to ensure the paint is the right thickness. Then the painter chooses the best equipment for the job, such as spray guns, airbrushes, roller brushes, or stencils.

It is important that industrial painters perform regular maintenance on their painting equipment. For example, painters who work in paint booths should regularly check the air filters to ensure the air quality is safe. They must follow the appropriate guidelines for safe handling of the products they use, as well as how to safely dispose of hazardous chemicals and waste.

While they work, industrial painters wear eye protection and coveralls, as well as face masks to prevent them from breathing in the chemicals that are in the paint.

A spray gun is used to cover large areas of plastic or metal, and is either attached directly to a container of paint or a long hose.

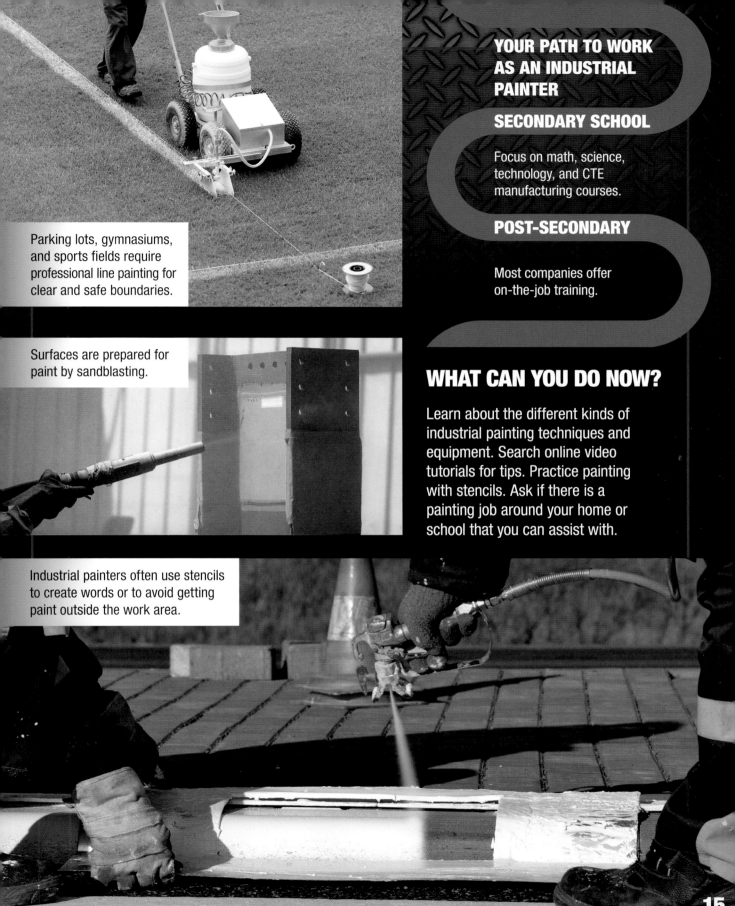

Parking lots, gymnasiums, and sports fields require professional line painting for clear and safe boundaries.

Surfaces are prepared for paint by sandblasting.

Industrial painters often use stencils to create words or to avoid getting paint outside the work area.

YOUR PATH TO WORK AS AN INDUSTRIAL PAINTER

SECONDARY SCHOOL

Focus on math, science, technology, and CTE manufacturing courses.

POST-SECONDARY

Most companies offer on-the-job training.

WHAT CAN YOU DO NOW?

Learn about the different kinds of industrial painting techniques and equipment. Search online video tutorials for tips. Practice painting with stencils. Ask if there is a painting job around your home or school that you can assist with.

DESIGN
ENGINEER

If you have a great imagination and want to pursue a career in which you can use your creativity as well as engineering principles, then look no further than design engineering.

ON THE JOB

Design engineers design new products that have yet to be put on the market, as well as machinery, equipment, and various types of mechanical systems. They also alter existing devices in order to improve the way they function. For example, a design engineer may modify a car's engine in order to improve its fuel efficiency. Once a design engineer has an idea for a product, he or she uses CAD software to create a technical design. A **prototype** of the model is made, which is tested for how well it functions. If the product needs more work, it is redesigned and modified until it is ready for the public to use.

Design engineers are creative thinkers. They think of new products that can help improve people's lives.

A design engineer uses CAD software to develop a mechanical device. A prototype based on this design will then be made.

YOUR PATH TO WORK AS A DESIGN ENGINEER

SECONDARY SCHOOL

Math, science, computer, technology, and CTE engineering or manufacturing courses are a great start.

POST-SECONDARY

A university degree in engineering, business development, or a related field is required.

WHAT CAN YOU DO NOW?

Think of a new product you would like to make. Plan out each step that would be required to make this product. Try making a prototype of the product and asking family and friends to help you test it. Search online for activities or tutorials that can help you with your product design. Join a young engineers' club or start one of your own.

DID YOU KNOW?

In 1973, Steve Jobs was an 18-year-old job seeker. On an application form, under special abilities, Jobs listed design engineer. A few years later, he cofounded Apple.

Design engineers work with a team of other engineers and designers to create innovative ideas. They must have strong problem-solving skills to improve on designs and models.

PIPEFITTER

Pipefitters, also known as steamfitters, work with piping systems that must withstand high pressure and move liquids and gases in factories and power plants.

ON THE JOB

Pipefitters assemble, maintain, and repair complex piping systems that carry steam, water, chemicals, and fuel. These piping systems include heating and cooling systems, as well as systems that are used in the manufacturing of products. To work as a pipefitter, you need a good understanding of engineering and mathematics. They study blueprints to determine what tools to use and the appropriate size and type of pipe for the job before measuring and cutting metal, such as carbon and stainless steel, and welding them together. When the pipes are ready, they transport them to the job site and install them. Pipefitters use special equipment to test piping systems for leaks and perform maintenance work on existing systems.

Pipefitters may be called to a site at any time. Problems with piping systems could cause a manufacturing plant to stop functioning.

WHAT CAN YOU DO NOW?

The next time a family member or trusted adult has a do-it-yourself project planned involving pipes, ask if you can assist. Research pipefitting techniques and processes online. Look for video tutorials to expand your knowledge.

DID YOU KNOW?

The Ontario Youth Apprenticeship Program (OYAP) provides high school students with opportunities to train in CTE careers. Students begin their apprenticeship training while completing their high school diploma.

YOUR PATH TO WORK AS A PIPEFITTER

SECONDARY SCHOOL

Math, science, technology, and CTE manufacturing courses are good preparation.

POST-SECONDARY

A college program and apprenticeship is required.

Pipefitters can be exposed to potentially harmful gases. They must wear personal protective equipment while they work, including respirators or masks.

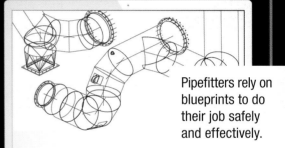

Pipefitters rely on blueprints to do their job safely and effectively.

According to the U.S. Bureau of Labor Statistics, more than 82,000 new pipefitters will be needed in the United States by 2022.

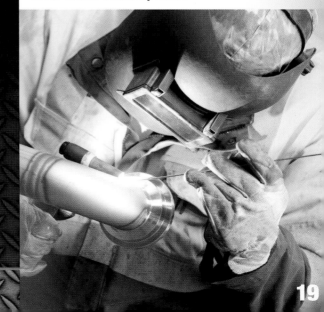

BOILERMAKER

ilermakers will always be in demand, since me boilers, which are vessels that heat ter under extreme pressure to produce ctricity, are used for more than 50 years.

A boilermaker manufactures, installs, and repairs boilers, tanks, and vats. Not only do boilers generate electricity, but steam and hot water from the boilers are also used to heat homes, factories, and even ships and swimming pools. Tanks and vats are storage containers for liquids such as chemicals, oils, and alcohol. The containers that boilermakers work on are made of steel, copper, and iron, so they must use hand and power tools and welding machines to cut the pieces and join them together.

These huge containers are used to store milk.

ON THE JOB

As a boilermaker, you will need to understand how to read blueprints to determine the boilers' part dimensions and their locations. Once the parts are fabricated, you will assemble them often with robotic or automatic welders. For boilers that have already been manufactured, you will be required to install them into buildings and factories. Boilermakers clean vats and tanks using cleaning **solvents**, wire brushes, and scrapers, and they must be able to find solutions to any defects they may find. You will be responsible for inspecting boiler **valves**, fittings, and water and **pressure gauges**, and make any necessary repairs. Boilermakers spend many hours on their feet and lift and move heavy components for the boilers and vats. Many boilermakers travel to different worksites and so must live away from home.

The job of a boilermaker can be physically demanding. The inside of boilers can be dark, damp, and cramped. Boilermakers often work outdoors, in all types of weather, and sometimes at great heights.

WHAT CAN YOU DO NOW?

Learn about the techniques and processes of boilermakers and the different kinds of boilers. Search for online videos showing boilermakers in action.

This gas boiler is part of a building's heating system.

YOUR PATH TO WORK AS A BOILERMAKER

SECONDARY SCHOOL

Focus on math, science, technology, and CTE manufacturing courses.

POST-SECONDARY

On-the-job training and apprenticeship programs are available.

DID YOU KNOW?

The Technology Student Association (TSA) is an organization for U.S. CTE students. It offers competitions and scholarships.

These boilermakers are repairing a piece of ship equipment.

INDUSTRIAL MAINTENANCE MECHANIC

Industrial maintenance mechanics, also known as toolsetters, are an important part of the manufacturing process. Without them, the machinery used to manufacture products would not be able to run!

ON THE JOB

Today, in addition to manual labor, the manufacturing industry uses machines and equipment to create products. To ensure everything is working as it should, industrial maintenance mechanics are needed to perform inspections and make any necessary repairs. When minor repairs are needed, such as replacing a broken part on a conveyor belt, mechanics can quickly fix the problem on-site so that production can continue to run. If a major breakdown on a machine occurs, mechanics must investigate the problem by referencing industrial drawings and manuals in order to dismantle, repair, and reassemble the machine.

Industrial maintenance mechanics often work in awkward positions, in cramped positions, or on top of ladders. To ensure their safety, they must follow safety procedures and wear personal protective equipment, such as steel-toed shoes and hardhats, and sometimes safety goggles.

THE WORKPLACE

If you decide to work as an industrial maintenance mechanic, you will have many options as to where you can work. In the past, mechanics used to specialize in one particular area, such as electronics, but today, many factories and plants hire mechanics who understand **hydraulics**, computer programming, and electricity. Having all of these skills will allow you to work on a broad range of machinery for various companies. Many companies will also consult with you before purchasing new machinery and equipment.

WHAT CAN YOU DO NOW?

Get curious about machines! Research different kinds of machinery, both how they are made and how they work. If you have the opportunity (and permission), try taking apart a device or piece of machinery to see its interior components. Search online for videos of machinery being repaired. Learn as much as you can about robotics. Join a robotics club or start your own.

YOUR PATH TO WORK AS AN INDUSTRIAL MAINTENANCE MECHANIC

SECONDARY SCHOOL

Focus on math, science, technology, and CTE manufacturing courses.

POST-SECONDARY

On-the-job training and apprenticeships are available.

DID YOU KNOW?

Industrial maintenance mechanics often train other employees, such as junior mechanics and **millwrights**, on machines. They also educate employees on the company's safety procedures.

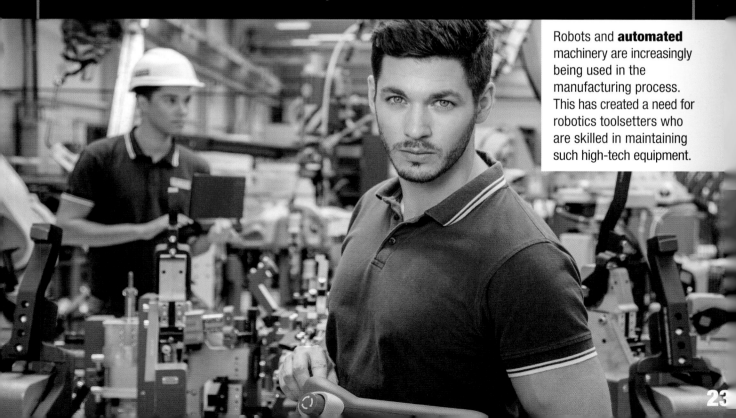

Robots and **automated** machinery are increasingly being used in the manufacturing process. This has created a need for robotics toolsetters who are skilled in maintaining such high-tech equipment.

QUALITY
CONTROL TECHNICIAN

Without quality control technicians, manufacturing products would be unsafe for all workers involved, and the products we use every day would not work as they are supposed to.

Quality control technicians make sure that the manufacturing process operates in an effective way. They check that machinery is working properly, and that the products being made meet the quality and safety standards of the company. As a quality control technician, you will be responsible for ensuring that employees follow the company's rules and guidelines, and that they receive the proper training to do their jobs well. When quality control technicians find a problem with a product, they are responsible for finding solutions, and keeping that product off the market until the problem is resolved.

Many governments have established quality standards for the manufacturing industry, including for companies that make children's toys. These standards help keep workers safe while they work, as well as ensuring the toys will be safe for children to play with them.

Pieces of machinery and equipment must meet certain **specifications** and standards to work safely and efficiently.

ON THE JOB

If you decide to become a quality control technician, you will be performing tests on materials and equipment while products are being made. This will give workers time to correct problems, which helps save time and money on wasted material. Once a product is completed, you will inspect it to make sure it meets quality standards. Quality control technicians record their data into computer spreadsheet programs in order to document their findings and to better understand how to make improvements.

WHAT CAN YOU DO NOW?

Become a quality control technician at home! Choose items in your home and inspect them for quality. Make a list of the **criteria** you are judging the items by and make notes as to why the item has or has not passed your inspection.

YOUR PATH TO WORK AS A QUALITY CONTROL TECHNICIAN

SECONDARY SCHOOL

Focus on math, science, computer, technology, and CTE manufacturing courses.

POST-SECONDARY

Certification is available from the American Society for Quality (ASQ), both in the U.S. and Canada.

DID YOU KNOW?

Sometimes, quality control technicians use X-rays and other sensor equipment to examine machines for problems.

Food and beverage companies take quality control very seriously, as the health and well-being of their customers depend on it. If a product is found to be unsafe, consumers will be less likely to trust that company or purchase its products.

LOGISTICS
ENGINEER

If you think that **logistics** engineers merely ship manufactured goods, you are wrong! These professionals use scientific and mathematical principles to make sure that goods are being distributed in the most efficient and profitable way possible.

The job of a logistics engineer is a complex but rewarding one. Logistics engineers organize the transportation, storage, and distribution of goods. They make sure that the product is where it is needed at the right time. As a logistics engineer, you will analyze and evaluate the methods used to accomplish this. Your goal will be to make improvements to the speed and cost of distributing goods, and you will need to focus on mathematics and science to do this.

By 2020, worldwide online sales are expected to reach $4.06 trillion. More and more warehouse are being built to store goods and keep up with demand.

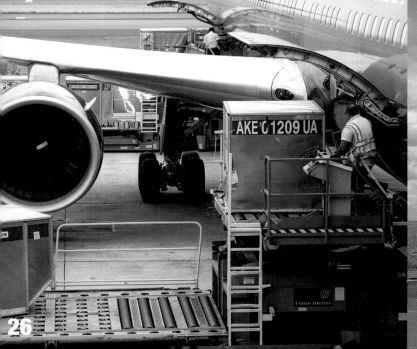

ON THE JOB

Logistics engineers work on the entire supply chain, which are the methods used to distribute a product, and so they have many job duties. They work with the inventory, or stock, of a product, plan the layouts of warehouses, and help to design the packaging of products in ways that will make shipping the product easier. If you decide to become a logistics engineer, you will need to understand the business relationship among the supplier of a product, the distributor, and the customer who will be using that product.

The International Society of Logistics and the American Production and Inventory Control Society (APICS) provide certification programs.

YOUR PATH TO WORK AS A LOGISTICS ENGINEER

SECONDARY SCHOOL

Focus on math, statistics, science, computer, technology, social studies, and CTE manufacturing courses.

POST-SECONDARY

A college or university degree in a related field is recommended.

WHAT CAN YOU DO NOW?

Get planning! Give yourself challenges to develop your logistics skills. What would be the best way to get your whole class to an amusement park for the whole day? Write out a list of steps the outing would require.

ENVIRONMENTAL
ENGINEER

ortunately, the manufacturing industry
ates a lot of waste and pollution.
ou are interested in protecting our
er, air, and soil from the effects of
ustry, you will appreciate the career
n environmental engineer.

ON THE JOB

An environmental engineer is an expert in
the branch of engineering that focuses on
reducing waste and pollution in order to protect
the environment. One of their duties is to focus
on ways to improve the quality of air, soil, and

water that has been contaminated
by harmful chemicals. Environmental
engineers also devise ways to control the
amount of pollution that is released by
manufacturing companies. Some of these
methods include designing **scrubbers**
and waste management systems.

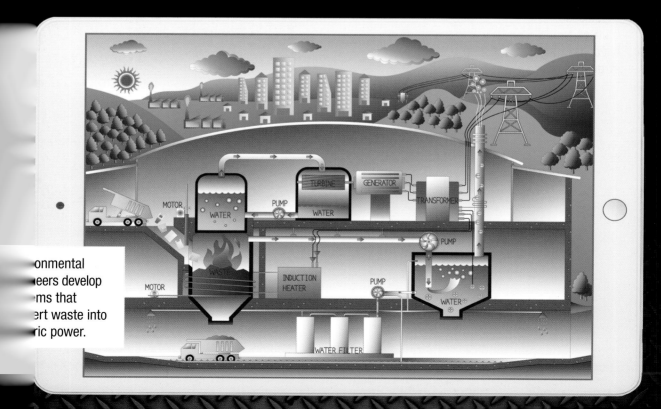

onmental
eers develop
ms that
ert waste into
ric power.

This engineer is checking the water quality at a wastewater treatment plant.

Environmental engineers often work at manufacturing plants. They conduct inspections of work practices and to coordinate a company's waste management activities.

YOUR PATH TO WORK AS AN ENVIRONMENTAL ENGINEER

SECONDARY SCHOOL

Focus on math, statistics, science, computer, technology, social studies, and CTE manufacturing courses.

POST-SECONDARY

A university degree is required.

DID YOU KNOW?

In the 1880s, Ellen Henrietta Swallow Richards, an American environmental chemist, began testing the water quality in Massachusetts. She performed tests on more than 40,000 samples of local water bodies that were used as drinking water. After high levels of **chlorine** were found in the samples, Massachusetts developed its first modern sewage treatment plant. Richards was a pioneer in industrial chemistry and worked with many groups dealing with water supplies and public health problems.

WHAT CAN YOU DO NOW?

Research environmental threats and the organizations that are working to protect water, air, and soil. Join an environmental awareness club or start your own. Download an app such as iNaturalist and explore your local surroundings. Be aware of how your own actions affect the environment every single day.

LEARNING MORE

BOOKS

Cohn, Jessica. *Manufacturing and Transportation*. Facts on File, 2008.

Hustad, Douglas. *How Can We Reduce Manufacturing Pollution?* Lerner, 2016.

Sjonger, Rebecca. *Robotics Engineering and Our Automated World*. Crabtree, 2017.

WEBSITES

WWW.CAREERTECH.ORG/ MANUFACTURING
There are many other jobs within the manufacturing pathways that are not covered in this book. Visit to learn about other career options!

WWW.MYNEXTMOVE.ORG/ EXPLORE/IP
Visit this website to help summarize your interests.

WWW.CAREERTECH.ORG/ STUDENT-INTEREST-SURVEY
The career guidance tool will help you to identify your top three career clusters based on your answers to a survey.

WWW.SKILLSUSA.ORG
SkillsUSA is an organization that aims to help students excel in the workforce by providing educational programs, events, and competitions.

WWW.TSAWEB.ORG
The Technology Student Association (TSA) offers activities such as competitions and leadership opportunities to students of science, technology, engineering, and mathematics.

GLOSSARY

alloy A strong metal made by combining two or more metallic elements

apprentice Someone who is learning a skilled trade from a professional

assurance Confidence or certainty in a high level of quality

automated To make a process in a factory or office operate by machines or computers

certification Certificate that shows someone has achieved a certain level of skill and knowledge

chlorine A chemical element used as a bleach or disinfectant

criteria A standard by which something is judged

dimensions The measurements of an object, such as length, width, and height

drum A cylindrical container

hydraulic Operated using he pressure of a fluid such as oil

innovation A new idea, invention, or way of doing things

intermediate bulk container (IBC) A reusable container designed for the transport and storage of liquids such as checmicals

jig A device used to secure the position of tools during assembly

logistics A detailed plan for operations involving many people or locations

milling cutter A steel cutter used for shaping metal surfaces

millwright A person who installs, repairs, and maintains machinery

petrochemical A chemical that comes from petroleum or natural gas

petroleum A liquid mixture found in rocks that can be turned into fuel, such as gasoline

pressure gauge An instrument that reads the weight or force produced when elements push against each other

prototype The first model of something from which others are copied

raw materials Items from which something useful can be made

sandblast A strong blast of sand used to clean stone or metal surfaces

scrubber Devices used to filter the exhaust of harmful gases

solvent Something that causes something else to break down and disappear, such as water breaks down salt

specification A detailed description of the design and materials used to make something

sterile Free from bacteria or germs

survey To examine and record the features of an area of land

template A model to be copied

textile Fiber used to make cloth

valve A door or gate used to control the flow of liquids or gases

welding The process of joining pieces of metal together by heating and melting

INDEX